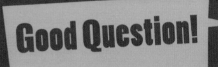

Good Question!

How Hot Is Lava?

AND OTHER QUESTIONS ABOUT . . .

Volcanoes

STERLING CHILDREN'S BOOKS
New York

STERLING CHILDREN'S BOOKS
New York

An Imprint of Sterling Publishing
1166 Avenue of the Americas
New York, NY 10036

Photo credits: 4: © Christian Goupi/SuperStock; 6: © Rainer Albiez/Shutterstock; 9: © Budkov Denis/Shutterstock; 16 left to right: © Peebles/Superstock, © Superstock; 17 left to right: © redbrickstock.com/Alamy, © Archive Farms/Getty Images, © Kerstin Langenberger/Superstock; 18: © Alberto Garcia/Corbis; 25: © Jonathan Blair/Corbis; 26: NASA; 29: © Carsten Peter/Corbis

ISBN 978-1-4549-1600-0 [hardcover]
ISBN 978-1-4549-1601-7 [paperback]

Distributed in Canada by Sterling Publishing
c/o Canadian Manda Group, 664 Annette Street
Toronto, Ontario, Canada M6S 2C8
Distributed in the United Kingdom by GMC Distribution Services
Castle Place, 166 High Street, Lewes, East Sussex, England BN7 1XU
Distributed in Australia by Capricorn Link (Australia) Pty. Ltd.
P.O. Box 704, Windsor, NSW 2756, Australia

Design by Andrea Miller
Art by Carol Schwartz

For information about custom editions, special sales, and premium and corporate purchases,
please contact Sterling Special Sales at 800-805-5489 or specialsales@sterlingpublishing.com.

Manufactured in China
Lot #:
2 4 6 8 10 9 7 5 3 1
12/15

www.sterlingpublishing.com/kids

CONTENTS

Can a volcano destroy an entire city?

A volcano *can* destroy an entire city. In fact, on August 24, in the year 79 CE a volcanic eruption destroyed *two* cities. In Italy, the volcano Mount Vesuvius erupted violently and buried the ancient Roman cities of Pompeii and Herculaneum. The deadly eruption lasted for two full days. Vesuvius spewed a mushroom cloud of gas, ash, and superheated rock that reached a height of 18 miles (30 kilometers). Southern winds blew the cloud over Pompeii, covering the city in darkness. Rock and ash rained down from the sky. Loud, terrifying sounds filled the air as the eruption blasted the earth apart. The ground shook, which caused some buildings to fall. More buildings collapsed under the weight of falling ash and rock. Lava from the eruption didn't travel far from the mouth of the volcano. More deadly than lava was the towering cloud of debris that collapsed under its own weight. The cloud's mixture of hot gas and rock flooded across both towns, burning everything in its path. By the time it was all over, Herculaneum was buried under 65 feet (20 meters) of rock and Pompeii was covered by nearly 16 feet (5 m) of debris. Both cities were hidden, like buried treasures, and forgotten for hundreds of years.

How do we know so much about this eruption that happened almost two thousand years ago? Both cities were uncovered—Pompeii in the late 1500s and Herculaneum in 1709. Once all the rock and ash were removed, people realized that the ancient Roman cities were remarkably well preserved. They had been sealed off from air and moisture when they were buried. Buildings, people, furniture, even bread baking in an oven, were all intact—frozen in time. Today, you can visit Pompeii and Herculaneum to see exactly what they looked like the day Vesuvius erupted.

When Pompeii was rediscovered, archaeologists made plaster casts of the bodies they uncovered.

This volcano on Stromboli Island in Italy erupts so often it's nicknamed the "Lighthouse of the Mediterranean."

What is a volcano?

You may think a volcano is a mountain that spews lava. But did you know that a volcano can be flat? In its simplest form, a volcano is a crack in the top layer of our planet that's so deep that melted rock from below can squeeze its way to the surface. To understand what's underneath that top layer, let's look at our home planet as a whole.

Planet Earth is made up of four different layers. The outer rocky layer where we live is called the crust. Miles beneath the crust is a layer of thick, hot, melted rock called the mantle. The final two layers are at the center of Earth. These layers are called the outer core and the inner core. The outer core is made of liquid metals, but the inner core is a solid, white-hot ball of metals. The temperature of the inner core is as hot as the surface of the sun—9,000 to 13,000 degrees Fahrenheit (5,000 to 7,000 degrees Celsius)! Pressure from the crust, mantle, and outer core keep the inner core packed into a solid sphere.

All that heat from the inner core causes the melted rock in the mantle to churn slowly like thick soup boiling in a pot. The crust sitting on top of the mantle is not a continuous layer. It's broken into large slabs called tectonic plates that float on top of the mantle. When melted rock from the mantle is able to rise up through cracks in Earth's crust, a volcano is born! When lava erupts out of a crack in the crust and cools, it can form the shape of a mountain—which is why we all tend to think of volcanoes as mountains that spew lava.

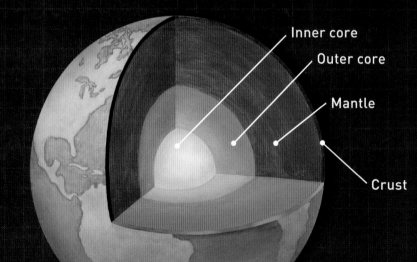

Inner core

Outer core

Mantle

Crust

What's the difference between magma and lava?

Magma is the mixture of melted, or molten, rock beneath the surface of Earth's crust. When magma breaks through the crust, it's called lava. There are three main types of lava: pahoehoe lava, a'a lava, and blocky lava. Pahoehoe (pa-hoy-hoy) lava is thin and pours out slowly like honey. As it spreads, the top layer cools to form a smooth skin while the red-hot bottom layer continues to flow. Eventually pahoehoe hardens into rounded ridges that look like tangled rope. A'a (ah-ah) lava is the opposite of pahoehoe. A'a is thick, like a milkshake blended with chunks of cookie. It forms a sharp, jagged crust as it cools. Blocky lava is even thicker and rougher than a'a. It's so heavy that it can't travel very far from the eruption site. It dries in a heap of large chunks.

How hot is lava?

The glowing red-orange lava that spills out of volcanoes can reach temperatures as high as 2,200°F (1,204°C). It's hard to imagine something so hot—the oven in your kitchen only goes up to about 500°F (260°C). Lava is so hot that it can destroy everything in its path. People have tried digging trenches, building concrete barriers, using water cannons to dump millions of gallons of cold water, and even dropping bombs on volcanoes to stop the flow of lava! Did any of it work? Not really, because lava is hard to predict.

Lava may be deadly and incredibly hot, but as soon as it hits the air it begins to cool. Once lava cools, it can form many different types of volcanic rock. If lava cools very quickly it can become a shiny, dark volcanic glass called obsidian, which Native Americans used to make arrowheads. If lava contains lots of gas, it can form a lightweight rock full of tiny holes called pumice. Thin lava can form a durable type of rock called basalt that is crushed and used to pave parking lots and roads.

Pahoehoe lava pours out of the Tolbachik volcano in Russia.

A Volcano Is Born

Convergent boundary

Hot spot

Divergent boundary

Subduction

Why do volcanoes spew lava?

Lava erupts when pressure forces molten rock to squeeze through cracks in Earth's crust. How does this happen? Sometimes, tectonic plates floating on top of the mantle crash into each other. The plates only move about 2 inches (5 cm) per year, but their massive size makes any collision very powerful. Crashing plates form what scientists call convergent boundaries. Pressure is created when two plates clash head-to-head. The collision causes one plate to bend and sink down beneath the other plate. This is called subduction. The sinking plate is pushed deep into the hot mantle where the rock melts and forms magma. Since magma weighs less than solid rock, it rises up beneath the crust, forming pools called magma chambers. If gas and pressure build in the chamber, magma will shoot up though a crack in Earth's crust, causing a volcanic eruption.

Volcanoes can also be created when two plates move away from each another. This is called a divergent boundary. The spreading plates create a gap in the crust, and magma rises up to the surface. Most divergent boundaries are found on the ocean floor. Lava seeping up through divergent plates created the mid-ocean ridge. This massive chain of underwater volcanic mountains circles the entire globe like the seam on a baseball. Seventy-five percent of all volcanic activity is hidden from view deep beneath the waves.

What is a hot spot?

All eight of the main Hawaiian Islands were formed by volcanic activity, but they are located in the *middle* of a tectonic plate. How can this be? Though most volcanoes occur at the edges of plates, hot spots are the exception to the rule. Hot spots form when magma surges up through the center of a plate and creates a volcano. Imagine a hot spot as a laser shooting up from the mantle and heating everything that passes over its beam of light. When a plate above a hot spot moves, new volcanoes are formed. Volcanoes that have drifted away from a hot spot are no longer active. Scientists estimate that there are forty to fifty hot spots across the world.

How many volcanoes are erupting right now?

Somewhere in the world, it's very likely that a volcano is erupting right now. Fifty to sixty volcanoes erupt each year. Some volcanoes start erupting and never stop. Mount Stromboli in Italy has been erupting almost continuously for the past two thousand years. Stromboli is an example of an active volcano. Scientists consider a volcano active if it is erupting, shows any signs that it might erupt, or has ever erupted in recorded history—that's a broad definition that includes 1,500 active volcanoes above sea level across the world. When a volcano isn't erupting now and shows no signs that it will erupt soon, we call it dormant. But a dormant volcano could still erupt in the future. An extinct volcano is one that scientists don't think will erupt again. Labeling a volcano extinct is a tough call since some volcanoes are millions of years old. The volcano in Yellowstone Park that causes the famous geyser Old Faithful is two million years old. It hasn't erupted in 70,000 years, but it's still not considered extinct.

Where is the Ring of Fire?

Three-quarters of the world's active and dormant volcanoes are located along the edges of a single tectonic plate in the Pacific Ocean called the Pacific Plate. The region is so explosive, it earned the name "Ring of Fire." The Ring of Fire is shaped like a horseshoe and includes 452 volcanoes—some are on land and some are underwater.

Ring of Fire

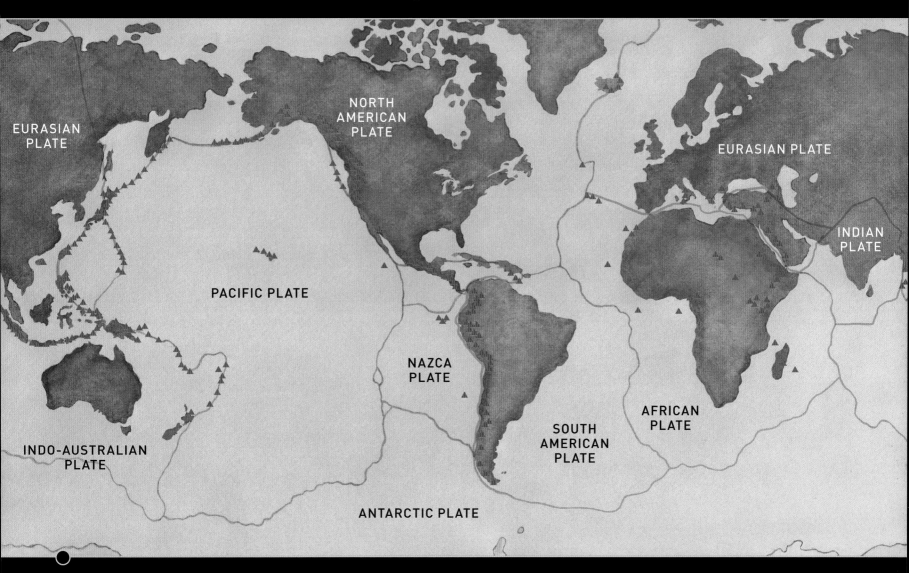

The red triangles on this map mark the locations of volcanoes. Most volcanoes can be found at the boundaries between two plates. Look at all the volcanoes surrounding the Pacific Plate— this is the "Ring of Fire."

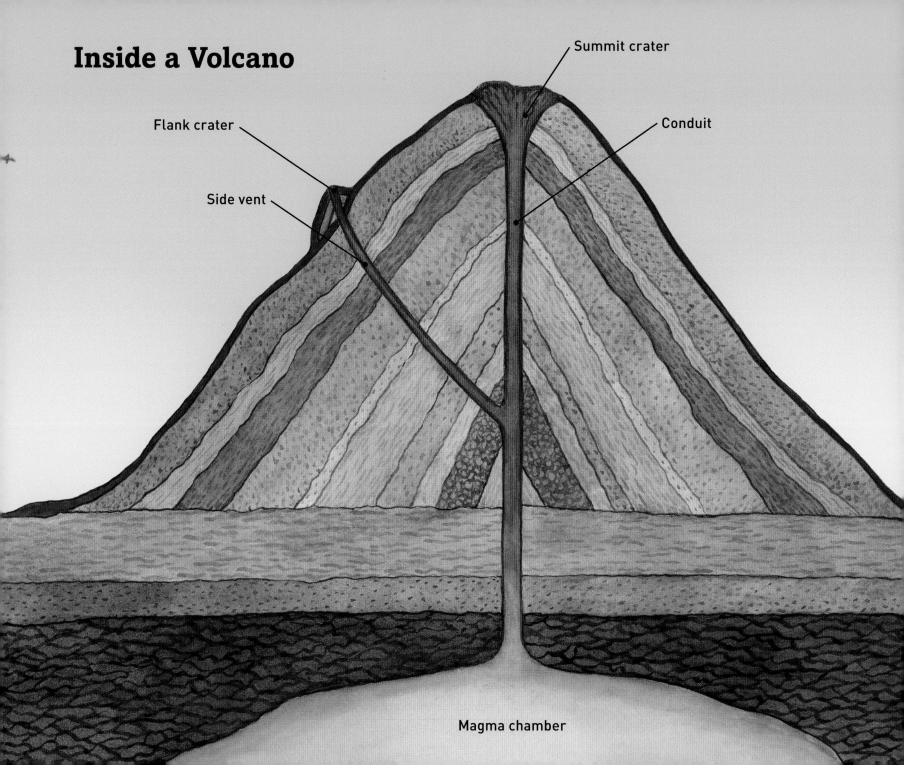

Inside a Volcano

Summit crater

Flank crater

Conduit

Side vent

Magma chamber

What's inside a volcano?

If it were possible to cut a volcano in half and peek inside, what would you see? At the base of the volcano, you'd find an underground magma chamber. A magma chamber is a pool of melted rock that seeped up from the mantle and collected in the crust. As pressure builds and the chamber fills with hot, liquid rock and gas, magma is driven up to the surface. The conduit is an escape route for magma—it's a central pipe inside the volcano that travels from the magma chamber to the surface. Some volcanoes have one conduit; others have a branching network of smaller conduits called side vents that carry magma to different sites along the slope of the volcano. When magma reaches the surface, it blasts or oozes out of bowl-shaped openings called craters. Craters located on the sides of volcanoes are called flank craters and craters located at the top are called summit craters.

Rare and beautiful lava lakes are formed when an eruption fills part of the summit crater with molten lava. The largest lava lake atop Mount Nyiragongo in Africa is 700 feet (213 m) across. Poisonous fumes and 1,800°F (982°C) heat make Mount Nyiragongo's lava lake dangerous, but so does the threat of a future eruption. In 2002, Nyiragongo erupted and emptied its lava lake onto the nearby city of Goma in a surge of lava that measured 656 feet (200 m) to 3,280 feet (1,000 m) wide and 6.5 feet high (2 m)! The city was evacuated before the deadly lava flooded in, but approximately 147 lives were still lost.

How many different ways can a volcano blow its top?

Some volcanoes erupt slowly and gently while others erupt violently. Volcanic eruptions can puff ash, steam, and smoke into the air or they can hurl chunks of molten rock as big as a house—a single eruption may even do both! Scientists have given names to the five different types of volcanic eruptions: Hawaiian, Strombolian, Vulcanian, Peléan, and Plinian.

Hawaiian eruptions spout a gentle, steady fountain of thin lava that spreads out over a wide area. Strombolian eruptions spew lava in mild bursts and sometimes toss ash and rock into the air. Vulcanian eruptions are like a cannon blast. When gas and pressure build beneath a thick, sticky plug of lava—*boom!*—thick clouds of ash and debris are shot high into the sky. Peléan eruptions are similar to Vulcanian eruptions, but Peléan eruptions can release clouds of hot gas and rock that collapse to form high-speed avalanches called pyroclastic flows. Plinian eruptions are the biggest of all. During a Plinian eruption, everything inside the volcano—gas, ash, and lava—can come roaring out in one tremendous explosion. Plinian eruptions can also cause pyroclastic flows that destroy everything for miles around.

Types of Volcanic Eruptions

HAWAIIAN

STROMBOLIAN

Volcanoes come in lots of different shapes and sizes, and you can tell how a volcano erupted in the past by looking at its shape. Fissure volcanoes are mostly flat. They are formed when a long crack in the Earth's crust churns out hot, fluid lava that spreads quickly. Shield volcanoes form low, broad slopes when thin lava pours out of the summit crater. Cinder cone volcanoes have steep slopes caused by eruptions of thick, clumpy lava that was too heavy to travel far from the crater. Composite volcanoes also have steep slopes, but they've been built up over time. Gentle lava flows followed by violent blasts create towering layers of debris—like a layered cake. Caldera volcanoes are formed when an eruption is so powerful that it collapses the peak of the volcano and forms a large shallow crater. Sometimes volcanic activity continues inside the crater—building the peak back up little by little.

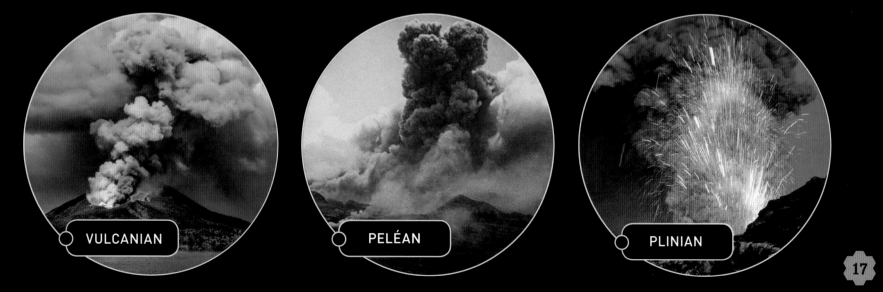

VULCANIAN

PELÉAN

PLINIAN

What makes volcanoes destructive and deadly?

I t's estimated that volcanic eruptions—and the damage they cause afterward—have killed more that 260,000 people in the past three hundred years. What makes them so deadly? Surprisingly, it's not lava. Even thin lava can travel only a few miles an hour. The range of lava's destruction is limited. Dramatic TV shows and movies make it look like lava is the biggest threat we face from volcanoes. But the deadliest and most destructive part of a volcanic eruption is often toxic gas and hot pieces of rock that mix to form a moving debris cloud called a pyroclastic flow. Imagine an unstoppable 1,000°F (538°C) avalanche of fiery rock and poisonous gas traveling at 300 mph (482 kph)! That's the power of a pyroclastic flow. Everything in its path is destroyed, burned, smashed, carried away, or buried. In 1902, the volcano Mount Pelée on the Caribbean island of Martinique erupted and the city of Saint Pierre was destroyed by a pyroclastic flow. Within minutes 29,000 people died. Only two people survived—Léon Compere-Léandre and Louis-Auguste Ciparis.

Compere-Léandre was a young shoemaker who survived because he was lucky enough to live on the edge of the pyroclastic flow. He reported, "I felt a terrible wind blowing, the earth began to tremble, and the sky suddenly became dark. I turned to go into the house . . . and felt my arms and legs burning, also my body. . . . My senses returned to me in perhaps an hour, when I beheld the roof burning. With sufficient strength left, my legs bleeding and covered with burns, I ran."

The other survivor, Louis-Auguste Ciparis, was badly burned as well. He was protected from the pyroclastic flow because he was a prisoner locked in a dungeon cell with only a small window. He was eventually pardoned for his crime and joined the circus! He toured with the Barnum and Bailey Circus telling his dramatic story and claiming to be the "Lone Survivor of Saint Pierre."

A car races away from the deadly pyroclastic flow unleashed by the eruption of Mount Pinatubo in 1991.

What were the biggest volcanic eruptions in history?

How do you measure a volcanic eruption? By how much stuff it spits out? By the height of its ash cloud? By how long the eruption lasts? The answer is all of the above and more. In 1982, scientists created a scale called the Volcanic Explosivity Index (VEI). The VEI ranks eruptions on a number scale from the weakest, 0, to the strongest, 8. There's a lot of debate about which eruptions are the "biggest." It's hard to say, but the following eruptions are famously gigantic.

▲ **Mount Tambora: VEI 7**

The 1815 eruption of Mount Tambora on the island of Sumbawa sent debris 27 miles (43 km) into the air. The ash cloud created total darkness for two days in the nearby area, and it also blocked sunlight all over the world. The year 1816 was called "the year without a summer." Ten thousand people were killed instantly by the eruption, but 100,000 more died of starvation when crops failed to grow without enough sunlight.

▲ **Krakatoa: VEI 6**

The 1883 eruption of the volcanic island of Krakatoa in Indonesia was twice as powerful as a nuclear bomb. The force of the explosion created terrifying 100-foot (30-m) waves that killed thousands of people on neighboring islands. The total death toll reached more than 36,000. The noise from the blast is the loudest sound ever heard. People 3,000 miles (4,800 km) away in Australia heard the eruption.

▲ **Mount Pinatubo: VEI 6**

On the crowded island of Luzon in the Philippines, Mount Pinatubo erupted in 1991 and started a chain reaction of wreckage. The powerful eruption sent enormous amounts of ash and toxic gas 22 miles (35 km) into the sky. Pyroclastic flows roared down and buried farmlands. The volcano collapsed causing earthquakes. At the same time, a typhoon hit the area, scattering ash everywhere. Water mixed with ash and created mudflows called lahars. Luckily, early evacuations saved many lives, but more than 1,000 people died and 650,000 were left homeless.

The eruption of Mount Tambora is the most destructive explosion on record in the past 10,000 years.

Did early volcanic eruptions help form our planet?

Volcanic eruptions can destroy parts of our planet, but they also helped to shape and form it. Eighty percent of Earth's surface was created by volcanic activity. Volcanoes have created beautiful mountains and fertile fields of soil that we use to grow food. But volcanoes are responsible for even more than the earth under our feet.

Volcanoes have been active for millions of years. Gases from early volcanic eruptions helped to form our atmosphere—the mixture of gas that surrounds our planet—as well as our oceans. Volcanoes provided, in part, the delicate balance of water and essential chemicals that mixed with energy from sunlight to create life on our planet. Volcanoes are an incredible force for both destruction and creation.

What is the largest volcano on Earth?

The largest volcano on Earth is called Tamu Massif and it's hidden about 4 miles (6 km) underwater in the Pacific Ocean. What Tamu Massif lacks in height (14,620 feet/4,460 m), it makes up for in width. It's approximately as wide as the state of New Mexico (120,000 square miles/310,799 square km). Located 1,000 miles east of Japan, Tamu Massif is thought to be 145 million years old. Luckily for us, it became extinct soon after it formed.

The largest active volcano and one of the tallest mountains on Earth is Mauna Loa, located on the big island of Hawai'i. It's been erupting on and off for the past 700,000 years and has grown to a total height of 10.5 miles (17 km)—2.5 miles (4 km) are above sea level and 8 miles (13 km) are below. Mauna Loa's eruptions are fueled by a hot spot. The chain of Hawaiian Islands were made by this same hot spot over millions of years. But, like all tectonic plates, the Pacific Plate that is home to Mauna Loa is on the move. It's estimated that Mauna Loa will drift away from the Hawaiian hot spot and become extinct 500,000 to one million years from now.

Earth, however, is not home to the largest volcano.

The largest volcano in the solar system. Turn the page to find out where it is!

Mauna Loa

Tamu Massif

Massive Mauna Loa is one of
Earth's most active volcanoes.

Olympus Mons

The largest volcano in the solar system is called Olympus Mons and it's located on our neighboring planet, Mars. Mars is usually red, but in this photo false colors have been added to show the elevation, or height, of Olympus Mons.

Are there volcanoes on other planets?

The largest volcano in the solar system is Olympus Mons located on our neighboring planet, Mars. Olympus Mons is so large that it can be seen from Earth with a high-powered backyard telescope. The massive Martian shield volcano rises 16 miles (25 km) high and is approximately the size of the state of Arizona. Scientists don't think Olympus Mons has been active for millions of years, but, surprisingly, some won't rule out the possibility of future eruptions. Olympus Mons is considered dormant but not extinct.

Earth and Mars aren't the only planets with volcanoes. Mercury, Venus, Earth's moon, and the moons of other planets are also home to volcanoes. Thick clouds make it hard to see the surface of Venus, but we know that it has more volcanoes than any other planet in our solar system. Mysterious Venus may have at least 100,000 volcanoes and maybe as many as one million! Scientists are still trying to figure out if any of Venus's volcanoes are active.

The most volcanically active place in the solar system is Io. Io is one of Jupiter's moons and is about the same size as Earth's moon. The unmanned spacecraft *Voyager 1* captured images of a volcanic eruption on Io in 1979. The Io eruption blasted a cloud of gasses and dust 190 miles (305 km) high. Since then, we've discovered that Io's surface is constantly being reshaped by volcanic activity.

Do we know when a volcano will erupt?

Earth scientists called volcanologists are trained to study volcanoes. One important part of their job is to carefully monitor active volcanoes that are likely to erupt—especially ones that are located near cities. Each volcano is different, which makes predicting eruptions difficult. However, studying past eruptions has given volcanologists clues about how volcanoes often behave right before major eruptions.

What are some common eruption signals?

- When plates shift, they can cause earthquakes that lead to a volcanic eruption. Therefore, volcanologists use seismometers, tools that measure motion in the ground, to track earthquake activity near active volcanoes.

- If the land surrounding a volcano tilts or bulges, this can be a sign that lava, gas, or pressure is building in the magma chamber below the ground. Volcanologists measure the degree of tilt all around the volcano and look for changes.

- If a volcano is seeping a lot of gas, especially sulfur dioxide (SO_2) and carbon dioxide (CO_2), this might mean a blast is on the way. Special instruments "sniff" the air around volcanoes to check for high levels of gas.

Not all volcanoes cooperate though. Some explode with no advance notice. But many volcanoes will give one or more of these signals, and lives can be saved if the people in the area are evacuated early. Volcanologists are getting better at predicting eruptions every year, making it safer for us to visit and admire active volcanoes up close.

Brave volcanologists risk their lives to study volcanoes. Their work helps to keep us all safe.

Some of the world's biggest eruptions happened before humans were around to witness them. Scientists think the super volcano simmering beneath Yellowstone National Park erupted two million years ago and blanketed the western half of the United States in a foot of ash!

Approximately 1630 BCE: Mount Thera, Greece— Also called the Minoan eruption, scientists think this could have been the strongest volcanic eruption ever witnessed even though there are no written records. The VEI 7 eruption blew apart the island of Santorini and buried it in 100 feet (30 m) of ash.

50 CE Ambrym Island, Republic of Vanuatu—This tiny volcanic island was the site of a BIG eruption—a VEI 6 that left a 7.5-mile (12 km) wide crater at the summit.

79: Mount Vesuvius, Italy—For more, see page 4.

450: Ilopango volcano, El Salvador—This VEI 6 explosion destroyed early Mayan cities, sent up enough ash to block the sun and cool the climate for more than a year, and may have killed more than one hundred thousand people instantly.

1000: Changbaishan volcano, at the border of China and North Korea—Also known as the Baitoushan volcano, it blew volcanic debris as far away as Japan during its VEI 7 eruption. The mountaintop is now a beautiful lake— Lake Tianchi.

1600: Huaynaputina volcano, Peru—With a VEI of 6, the eruption of Huaynaputina is the biggest on record in South America. It rivals the 1883 eruption of Krakatoa. Ash from its blast covered 20 square miles (50 square km) and changed the global climate.

1815: Mount Tambora, Indonesia—For more, see page 20.

1883: Krakatoa, Indonesia—For more, see page 20.

1902: Mount Pelée, Martinique—For more, see page 19.

1902: Santa Maria volcano, Guatemala—This colossal VEI 6 blast sent ash all the way to San Francisco, California.

1912: Novarupta volcano, United States—Rated VEI 6, this blast in Alaska was the largest of the twentieth century. It sent 3 cubic miles (12.5 cubic km) of magma and ash into the air and when it all finally settled it covered 3,000 square miles (7,800 square km) with more than a foot of ash.

1980: Mount Saint Helens, United States—The VEI 5 eruption of Mount Saint Helens in Washington State weakened the north face of the mountain until it crumbled, creating the largest landslide on record. The ash cloud climbed 15 miles (24 km) high.

1991: Mount Pinatubo, Philippines—For more, see page 20.

2010: Eyjafjallajökull volcano, Iceland—The series of eruptions in 2010 earned a VEI of 4, and their impact was vast. Eyjafjallajökull's ash cloud rose to a height of 30,000 feet (9 km), which was just the right height to block airplane travel across Europe—affecting ten million travelers.

FIND OUT MORE

Books to Read

Berger, Melvin and Gilda. *Why Do Volcanoes Blow Their Tops? Questions and Answers About Volcanoes and Earthquakes.* New York, NY: Scholastic Reference, 1999.

Branley, Franklyn M. *Let's-Read-and-Find-Out Science: Volcanoes.* New York, NY: Collins, 2008.

Carson, Mary Kay. *Good Question: Why Does Earth Spin? And Other Questions About . . . Our Planet.* New York, NY: Sterling Publishing, 2014.

Stewart, Melissa. *Inside Volcanoes.* New York, NY: Sterling Publishing, 2011.

Van Rose, Susanna. *Eyewitness Volcano & Earthquake.* New York, NY: Dorling Kindersley Limited, 2008.

Websites to Visit

CHECK OUT ALL THE VOLCANIC ERUPTIONS FROM THE PAST WEEK:
http://www.volcano.si.edu/reports_weekly.cfm

LEARN ABOUT PAST VOLCANIC ERUPTIONS:
http://www.volcano.si.edu/search_eruption.cfm

WATCH A VOLCANO WEBCAM:
http://volcanoes.usgs.gov/images/webcams.php

BUILD A VOLCANO:
http://www.nhm.ac.uk/kids-only/earth-space/volcanoes/build-a-volcano/

DO YOU WANT TO BECOME A VOLCANOLOGIST?
http://volcano.oregonstate.edu/oldroot/volcanologist/how_to.html

For bibliography and free activities visit: http://sterlingpublishing.com/kids/good-question

INDEX